HOW? WHO? WHAT? WHEN? WHERE? WHY?

ABOUT
CUSTOMS AND TRADITIONS

PUBLISHER	Joseph R. DeVarennes	
PUBLICATION DIRECTOR	Kenneth H. Pearson	
ADVISORS	Roger Aubin	
	Robert Furlonger	
EDITORIAL SUPERVISOR	Jocelyn Smyth	
PRODUCTION MANAGER	Ernest Homewood	
PRODUCTION ASSISTANTS	Martine Gingras	Kathy Kishimoto
	Catherine Gordon	Peter Thomlison
CONTRIBUTORS	Alison Dickie	Nancy Prasad
	Bill Ivy	Lois Rock
	Jacqueline Kendel	Merebeth Switzer
	Anne Langdon	Dave Taylor
	Sheila Macdonald	Alison Tharen
	Susan Marshall	Donna Thomson
	Pamela Martin	Pam Young
	Colin McCance	
SENIOR EDITOR	Robin Rivers	
EDITORS	Brian Cross	Ann Martin
	Anne Louise Mahoney	Mayta Tannenbaum
PUBLICATION ADMINISTRATOR	Anna Good	
ART AND DESIGN	Richard Comely	Ronald Migliore
	Robert B. Curry	Penelope Moir
	George Elliott	Marion Stuck
	Marilyn James	Bill Suddick
	Robert Johanssen	Sue Wilkinson

Canadian Cataloguing in Publication Data

Main entry under title:

Questions kids ask about customs and traditions

(Questions kids ask; 8)
ISBN 0-7172-2547-X

1. Manners and customs—Miscellanea—Juvenile literature.
2. Festivals—Miscellanea—Juvenile literature.
3. Holidays—Miscellanea—Juvenile literature.
4. Children's questions and answers.
I. Smyth, Jocelyn.   II. Comely, Richard.   III. Series.

GT85.Q48 1988   j390   C89-093161-5

Questions Kids Ask . . .
about CUSTOMS and TRADITIONS

continued

Why do we light candles on birthday cakes?

Long ago, people lit fires and whispered prayers to the gods
into the smoke. They watched the smoke travel up into the
sky and hoped that their prayers would be answered.
The ancient Greeks regarded birthdays, like birth, as a
time of danger. On their birthdays, Greek children
were given a tiny cake with a candle burning on it.
They asked the gods for protection and blew out the
candle. They, too, hoped that the smoke would
carry their message up to the gods.
We still put candles on a birthday
cake, but now people wish for whatever
they most want, blow out the candles,
and hope their wish
comes true!

Why do we paint eggs at Easter?

Eggs are a symbol of new life. Because Easter celebrates new life, early Christians exchanged decorated eggs as part of the Easter festivities. Wealthy people decorated eggs with gold, and even poor people dyed their eggs to make them more attractive.

In Russia, a hundred years ago, a goldsmith named Fabergé designed eggs that were works of art. Made with gold and precious jewels, these were gifts from the Czar of Russia to his wife. The Fabergé eggs are now kept in museums and private collections.

DID YOU KNOW . . . confetti is an Italian word meaning "sweets." Hundreds of years ago in Italy, people used to throw candies during celebrations. Someone started making paper candies from colored cardboard, which eventually led to confetti as we know it.

Why do people throw confetti at weddings?

Modern brides and grooms might be surprised to learn that many of the customs still practiced at weddings were started hundreds of years ago.

Long ago, wedding guests showered the bride and groom with rice or wheat after the wedding ceremony. These were symbols of fertility, and people tossed them at the newlyweds so that they would have a large family. Rice and wheat have been replaced by colorful paper confetti, but the reason for throwing it remains the same.

What is Hanukkah?

Hanukkah is a Jewish festival that usually takes place in December. Two thousand years ago, the Jews defeated their enemies, the Syrians, and drove them out of the Temple in Jerusalem. The Jews wanted to light holy lamps to thank God for bringing them victory, but they had only one pot of oil—not nearly enough to keep their lamps lit for long. Miraculously, the oil kept their lamps burning for eight days. A Jewish leader declared this a festival, now called the Festival of Lights, to be celebrated every year.

Today, Jewish children celebrate Hanukkah by lighting candles in a special nine-branch candlestick called a *menorah*. They light one candle a day for each of the eight days of Hanukkah to remember the miracle.

What was the first Christmas carol?

It is difficult to tell which Christmas carol is the oldest because some were never written down. "God Rest Ye Merry, Gentlemen" from England and "The First Noel" from France, both written in the 1500s, seem to be the oldest. No one is certain who wrote them.

We do know who wrote one of the most popular carols "Silent Night, Holy Night!" Joseph Mohr, the pastor of a small church in Austria, wrote the words on Christmas Eve in 1818. The church organist, Franz Gruber, composed the music and played it at midnight Mass—on a guitar. Mice had eaten holes in the church organ.

How did April Fool's Day begin?

*The first of April, some do say
Is set apart for All Fool's Day;
But why the people call it so
Nor I, nor they themselves,
    do know.*

From *Poor Robin's Almanac,* 1760

April Fool's Day is the first day of April. For centuries it has been the one day set aside each year for playing harmless tricks and pranks. Whoever is the butt of the joke is the April Fool.

The tradition started in France. In the early 1500s the French celebrated the New Year from March 21 until April 1. In 1564 the king adopted a new calendar, which changed New Year's Day to January 1. Some people refused to accept the new calendar and continued to celebrate New Year's Day on April 1. These people were called April Fools, and it became the custom to play tricks on them. They were sent ridiculous gifts, invited to parties that didn't exist, and made the butt of other such jokes and pranks. The custom of fooling people on April 1 has continued.

Most people just can't resist the chance to play a good joke!

Why is February 14th called Valentine's Day?

There are many legends concerning St. Valentine and Valentine's Day. After 1700 years, it's difficult to separate fact from fiction!

We do know that there was a priest named Valentine who lived in Rome in the third century. The emperor of that time had

When was the first Mother's Day?

In 1908, an American woman named Anna Jarvis wanted to do something special in memory of her mother. Exactly two years after her mother's death, she persuaded her local church to hold an annual service honoring all mothers. The first Mother's Day service was held the following year, on the second Sunday in May. The idea caught on, and the day was made official by the American government in 1914. Within a few years, nearly every country had a Mother's Day.

Anna Jarvis was very angry when people turned Mother's Day, which was originally a religious occasion, into a commercial event. They made money by selling cards, gifts and flowers.

If you decide to send a greeting card on Mother's Day, perhaps you should make it yourself!

forbidden his soldiers to marry, fearing that marriage would make them unsuited for fighting. Valentine married these soldiers to their sweethearts in secret. When he was caught, the emperor had him executed.

Over 200 years later, the Church of Rome replaced the pagan god of lovers, Lupercus, with the martyred St. Valentine.

The Lupercian festival of love became the feast of St. Valentine, now the patron saint of lovers.

Some people said that the sending of valentine cards was started by Valentine himself when he was in prison. Other people say that there is no connection between the two. However it started, the tradition of sending valentines is here to stay!

Where was the first Christmas tree?

Decorating a tree at Christmastime is a German tradition that goes back more than three centuries. Some claim that the idea belonged to a famous German churchman named Martin Luther. One night while walking in the woods, Martin knelt to pray. As he raised his eyes he saw the twinkling reflection of the stars on the snow-covered fir trees. Martin cut down one of the trees, dragged it back to his church, and decorated it with lit candles as a symbol of the sight of heaven he'd seen in the woods. The idea eventually became popular; decorated trees began to appear in German homes in 1605. The Germans brought this tradition to North America in the 1800s.

DID YOU KNOW . . . the first Christmas trees in North America were put on public exhibit, and people had to pay to see them!

Why do we hang stockings on Christmas Eve?

The tradition of hanging Christmas stockings was started in Holland. According to Dutch folklore, St. Nicholas, the protector of children, brought treats to all good girls and boys on December 6 (St. Nicholas Day). The night before this, Dutch children left a pair of wooden shoes on their doorsteps for him to fill with goodies.

One year, St. Nicholas heard of three girls who were so poor they didn't have any shoes. Instead of giving them toys, he threw three bags of gold down their chimney. The gold fell into their stockings, which hung by the fire to dry.

When Dutch families immigrated to North America, they brought the story of St. Nicholas and the stockings with them and made it part of Christmas. Ever since, people here who celebrate Christmas have hung stockings from the mantel on Christmas Eve for St. Nicholas, also known as Santa Claus, to fill with presents.

Why is December 26th called Boxing Day?

The day after Christmas is called Boxing Day and it is also known as St. Stephen's Day. St. Stephen was the patron saint of the poor. On that day, it was the custom to give food, clothing and money to poor people. Because these donations were packed in boxes, the day got the nickname ''Boxing Day.''

Why do kings and queens wear crowns?

A long time ago, it was believed that kings and queens were very different from other people. Royalty supposedly had special powers and might even be gods or goddesses!

Rulers wore clothes that were different from everyone else's. They had special objects—such as scepters, robes, thrones and crowns—that no one else had. The rulers' subjects believed that these objects helped the rulers keep their powers. In ancient Egypt it was thought that the crowns actually contained power, and that the crowns or head-dresses helped link their rulers to gods and goddesses.

Over thousands of years and different cultures, many types of head-dresses and crowns have been worn by royalty. Some were simple bands of cloth or metal called *diadems*. Modern crowns are like these early diadems, except now they are made of precious metals and often are decorated with jewels.

Today we know that kings and queens are not that different from the rest of us—they simply have a different job to do. They still wear crowns on special occasions, but we value the tradition of wearing a crown more than its original meaning.

14

Why do people wear rings?

The custom of wearing rings is probably as old as the human race, but the earliest rings were found in the tombs of ancient Egypt. People today wear different rings for different reasons. Some rings are a sign of authority, such as the pope's ring. Each pope is given a new ring, called the fisherman's ring, because it bears a picture of St. Peter in a boat.

Rings are also a symbol of love or marriage. The Romans were probably the first to use engagement and wedding rings. Wedding rings are usually worn on the third finger of the left hand because of an old, but untrue, belief that a vein runs directly from this finger to the heart.

Of course, there are also many, many rings that have no special significance. They're simply worn as ornaments.

Can there ever be a blue moon?

You may have heard people say that something only happens "once in a blue moon." This means it happens once in a lifetime, or very rarely. Many people think it's just an old saying, but the truth is there can be a blue moon!

The moon looks blue when dust from a volcano mixes with smoke from forest fires. As you may know, light is made up of the seven different colors you see in a rainbow, and each color has a different wavelength. The particles of the mixture of dust and smoke are the right size to scatter the red waves in the moonlight but not the blue ones, which are shorter. Because you can see the blue rays better than usual, the moon appears to be blue. According to astronomical studies, this happens about once every 70 to 80 years!

Does a full moon make you wacky?

Since earliest times, people have been awed by the sight of a full, glowing moon. Early people thought the moon was a powerful god or goddess. The idea that a full moon makes you wacky comes from an old superstition that sleeping under a full moon could cause a person to go insane.

In fact, the word "lunatic" comes from *luna,* the Latin word for moon. It was thought that a lunatic was someone who had been moon-struck. Periods of insanity were thought to depend on changes in the moon's cycle.

But don't worry. A full moon doesn't make you wacky—it's just a superstition.

How did nightmares get their name?

Did you think nightmares had something to do with horses? Today, the word "mare" does mean a female horse, but in the past it was the word for an evil spirit. People believed that from time to time the evil spirit, or *maere,* came and sat on their chest at night, making them feel as if they were suffocating. When people had a terrifying dream, they said they had been visited by the "nightmare."

How do Chinese people celebrate the New Year?

Although China follows the same calendar that we do, their New Year doesn't start on January 1. The date of the Chinese New Year changes every year, because it takes place on the date of the second new moon after the winter solstice (the time when the sun is farthest from the equator). The festival usually occurs between January 21 and February 19.

The celebration can last for up to 15 days. On the day before New Year's Eve, people visit their friends and neighbors to wish them well. The next day, each family has a New Year's Eve feast. All the doors are sealed with paper so no evil spirits can get in. People exchange gifts after the meal, and at midnight have their own family celebrations. On New Year's Day the Lantern Festival takes place, and parades with paper lanterns and long, dancing dragons wind through the streets.

Why do people blow horns on New Year's Eve?

Do you believe in evil spirits? The Celtic people who lived more than 2000 years ago in the areas that are now France, Britain and Ireland did. They celebrated New Year's Eve on October 31. This was the night of of festivities in honor of ''Samhain,'' Lord of the Dead, and the night they believed evil spirits stalked the earth. At midnight, people would bang rocks, yell, blow horns and make as much noise as they could to scare off the spirits—they didn't want them hanging around in the New Year.

When Christianity was introduced, the date for the New Year was set for January 1, seven days after the birth of Christ. But, in the tradition of the ancient Samhain festival, people continued to make noise at the stroke of midnight.

The custom is still with us, although probably few people know how it started.

Who is Jack Frost?

The people who lived in Norway hundreds of years ago believed in gods who brought the cold winter weather. One of the gods was named Jokul, which meant icicle, or Frosti, which meant frost. This gave us the English name Jack Frost. Today, people think of Jack as the little sprite who draws lovely patterns of frost on windows and trims the grass and trees with ice.

Why do we shake hands?

Did you know that when you shake hands with someone you're really saying "I'm friendly"?

During the Middle Ages, strangers sometimes approached each other with their arms outstretched. They did this to show that they had no weapons. This demonstration of "friendliness" is believed to have been the origin of the handshake.

Less than 100 years ago, people entered important business deals with only a handshake. By shaking hands they each promised that they would follow an agreement and not break it.

Today business deals are put down in writing. It's still the custom, however, to "seal" a deal by shaking hands in a show of friendly intentions.

Where do surnames come from?

Your surname is your last name, which you share with other members of your family. There are many different ways that surnames came to be.

The Vikings were among the first people to use surnames. They added their father's name to their given name. For example, Eric's son Leif was called Leif Ericson. Leif's son Harold would be called Harold Leifson, and Leif's daughter Kristin was Kristin Leifsdatter. This became too complicated, so people chose one surname to pass on.

Another form of surname came from the type of business the family was in. David the Tailor was shortened to David Tailor.

Some surnames came from where a person lived. If a man lived on a hill, he would be called Mr. Hill. Surnames such as Wood, Brooks and Stone started this way.

Why do people kiss the Blarney Stone?

Have you ever kissed a rock? Thousands of people travel to Ireland every year and do just that.

The Blarney Stone is a big block of limestone in Blarney Castle near the city of Cork, in Ireland. Legends tell about the owner of the castle who would flatter his enemies so they wouldn't attack.

It is said that whoever kisses the stone will be given the power to sweet-talk people, just like the owner of the castle could. Kissing the stone is not easy—you have to lean backwards over a ledge to reach it!

DID YOU KNOW . . . if you can talk people into doing what you want, you are said to have "the gift of blarney."

Why do Japanese people remove their shoes inside the house?

In traditional Japanese homes, there is very little furniture. People sit cross-legged on the floor at a low table to eat, and unroll soft mattresses on the floor to sleep on each night. Since

Why do people knock on wood?

How many times have you heard someone say something and then add "knock on wood"?

This superstition dates back to the days when people believed that gods lived in trees. If they spoke of good fortune that had come their way or of something good they hoped would happen, they knocked on a tree as a way of saying "thank you" or "please" to the gods.

People today are not so serious about superstitions, but they still laughingly say "knock on wood" —and sometimes even do it. They hope it will help make something they're wishing for come true.

Thank you...

people sit and sleep on the floor, Japanese customs insist that everyone remove their shoes when they enter a house so that the floor does not get dirty. It is considered very bad manners to leave your shoes on in a traditional Japanese home, just as it would be if you walked all over your family's furniture in your shoes!

Are there such things as jinxes and curses?

The idea that someone or something can be cursed is as old as culture itself. In fairytales a curse was called a magic spell and was usually cast by a wicked old witch. In real life you've probably heard it said that an object or person who has had a series of misfortunes is "jinxed."

A jinx or curse is said to bring bad luck or even death to the person it has been put on. Some people believe that curses can be placed on others by casting spells, or by chanting certain words. Although there are thousands of stories that make it look as if jinxes and curses do exist, there is no scientific evidence that they have been the cause of any harm.

Does breaking a mirror bring bad luck?

An old superstition claims that breaking a mirror brings seven years of bad luck.

Ancient people believed that if you saw your reflection, you left part of your soul behind when you turned away. The earliest mirrors were pools of water, and pools don't break. But glass mirrors do, and when they were invented, people feared that their soul would be lost if the glass were to break.

Why would the bad luck last seven years? That was also an ancient belief. People once thought that the body and mind changed completely every seven years. At the end of each seven-year cycle, the soul and body came together again for a new beginning. So, seven years after breaking the mirror, your soul would be returned to you, and you could start a new cycle.

Why is Friday the 13th thought to be unlucky?

Thirteen is said to be an unlucky number. Many people will not have 13 people at a dinner party, and many tall buildings do not have a floor numbered "13."

But why is this number unlucky? People long ago looked upon 13 as the number of death because there were 13 people at the Last Supper—Christ and his 12 apostles.

Friday is also considered unlucky, probably because Christ was crucified on a Friday. So when the 13th day of a month falls on a Friday, superstitious people claim it's double bad luck!

DID YOU KNOW . . . there is even a name for the fear of number 13—triskaidekaphobia!

DID YOU KNOW . . . only one person in seven in the world eats with a fork. Nearly twice as many use chopsticks and the rest use their fingers!

When did people begin eating with forks?

How did people eat before they used forks?

Many ate with their fingers, others speared food with two knives, and some used a spoon. Although two-pronged forks did exist, anyone who used one was thought to be very finicky and affected.

It was less than 300 years ago that forks came into fashion. In France they became a status symbol and a luxury, used only by the upper classes. By the end of the 18th century, the idea had spread across Europe and forks could be found on the table in most European homes.

Who invented table manners?

Table manners have been around for a long time—at least 4500 years. It was not until about 800 years ago, however, that books on this subject were published. In one of the first books on manners, people were told not to spit on or over the dinner table!

Good table manners separated the upper classes from the lower classes of society. In some countries, the rich only used three fingers to eat with, while poorer people used all five. Strict rules of etiquette were followed by royalty and aristocrats; everyone else used more relaxed rules.

Table manners are still with us today, but they have changed somewhat over the years—250 years ago, your mother would have told you to wipe your dirty hands on some bread before using your napkin!

Why do people dress up on Hallowe'en?

On October 31, the streets are filled with trick-or-treaters. Disguised in costumes and masks, children go from door to door and neighbors fill their bags with goodies.

Dressing up on Hallowe'en is a very old custom that began with people called Celts. The Celts lived more than 2000 years ago in what is now Great Britain, Ireland and northern France.

The Celtic New Year began on November 1, a day that also marked the beginning of winter—the season of cold, darkness and death. On October 31, the eve of winter, the Celts held the festival of Samhain, the Celtic lord of death.

The Celts believed that on this night Samhain allowed ghosts to rise from their graves. They were joined by demons, goblins and others. Priests built a bonfire believing that the burning branches would keep the evil spirits away. They tossed food and animals into the flames as sacrifices to keep Samhain happy so *he* would stay away. People gathered around the fire, many in costumes made of animal heads and skins as further protection against evil spirits.

Even after the Celts became Christians, they still celebrated this festival. The Christian Church finally decided to make November 1 a Christian holy day, calling it All Hallows or Saints' Day. October 31 thus became All Hallows Eve(n)—or Hallowe'en.

How did the jack-o'-lantern get its name?

We have the Irish to thank for the name "jack-o'-lantern." According to an early 19th-century Irish folktale, a tricky fellow named Jack was such a sinner that he was turned back at the gates to heaven. Jack made his way to hell, but the devil wouldn't have him either.

"Go back to where you came from!" the devil shouted.

"How will I find my way back in the dark?" Jack asked. Instead of answering, the devil tossed him a burning coal. Jack put the coal inside a hollowed-out turnip and used it as a lantern.

Every Hallowe'en, the story goes, Jack can be seen roaming the earth with his lantern. To this day, we carve out pumpkins and light candles inside them to scare off evil spirits who come out on Hallowe'en. Thanks to Jack, they're called jack-o'-lanterns.

Does tying a string around your finger help you remember things?

Hundreds of years ago, many people tied a string around their finger when they had a good idea. They thought that the string would keep the idea from escaping.

You may still see people with string tied around their fingers, but today it means "don't forget." The string is a reminder that there is something to remember. But what if you forget why you put the string there?

Is it bad luck to walk under a ladder?

Ancient peoples were afraid to walk under ladders because they thought that gods lived in the triangle-shaped space underneath. For someone to walk through a sacred place like this was very disrespectful to the gods.

Early Christians considered the ladder a symbol of wickedness because a ladder had led up to Christ's crucifix, and so walking under a ladder was bad luck.

Today some superstitious people still avoid walking under ladders for fear of bad luck. And so do many people who are not superstitious but who fear that some clumsy person at the top will drop something on them!

DID YOU KNOW . . . the famous British admiral Lord Nelson had a horseshoe nailed to the mast of his ship, *Victory*.

Do horseshoes bring good luck?

Have you ever been told that it's lucky to find a horseshoe? This belief comes from 4th-century Greece. A horseshoe is crescent-shaped like the new moon, which was a symbol of good luck and fertility. Also, horseshoes are made of iron, which was thought to ward off evil. A horseshoe nailed over a doorway supposedly kept witches and other evil spirits from entering the house. For extra protection, it was said the horseshoe must be fixed with the ends pointing up, or all the good luck would drain out of it!

Index _____